Rookie
Read-About® Science

From Seed
to Plant

By Allan Fowler

Consultant
Janann V. Jenner, Ph.D.

Property of
Lisa Efthymiou

Children's Press®
A Division of Grolier Publishing
New York   London   Hong Kong   Sydney
Danbury, Connecticut

Designer: Herman Adler Design Group
Photo Researcher: Caroline Anderson
The photo on the cover shows a plant sprouting from a seed.

Library of Congress Cataloging-in-Publication Data

Fowler, Allan.
    From seed to plant / by Allan Fowler.
      p. cm. — (Rookie read-about science)
    Includes index.
    Summary: Describes the development of a seed into a plant by means
of pollination, fertilization, and seed dispersal.
    ISBN 0-516-21682-1 (lib. bdg.)   0-516-27307-8 (pbk.)
    1. Seeds—Juvenile literature. 2. Plants—Development—Juvenile
literature. [1. Seeds. 2. Plants—Development.] I. Title. II. Series.
QK661.F58   2001
581.4'67—dc21
                                     99-057024

Seeds are in a lot of the foods you eat.

4

Tomato seeds are tiny. You can swallow them and not even know it.

Watermelon seeds are too hard to swallow. You spit them out.

Peach pits are too big
to swallow. You eat
around them.

Seeds are important. All plants grow from seeds.

How do seeds form? They begin with tiny grains called pollen. Pollen is made in the stamens (STAY-mens) of a flower.

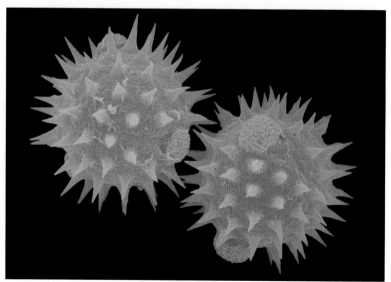

Pollen

Stamen

11

When a bee visits a flower
to sip its sweet nectar,
pollen clings to the insect's
body. When the bee visits
another flower of the same
kind, some pollen falls onto
that flower's pistil (PIS-til).

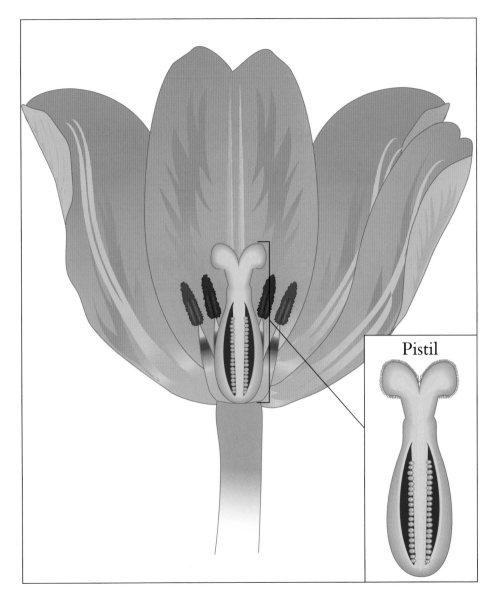

Pistil

At the bottom of the pistil,
a seedcase holds eggs.

Each pollen grain sends
a slender tube down the
pistil to the eggs.

One tube grows into each
egg in the seedcase.

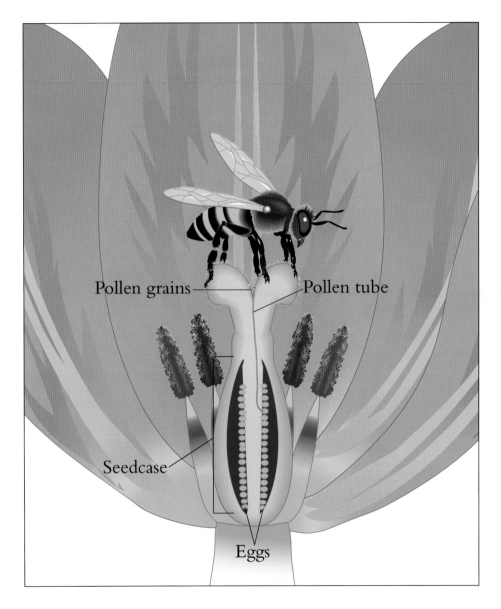

Pollen grains

Pollen tube

Seedcase

Eggs

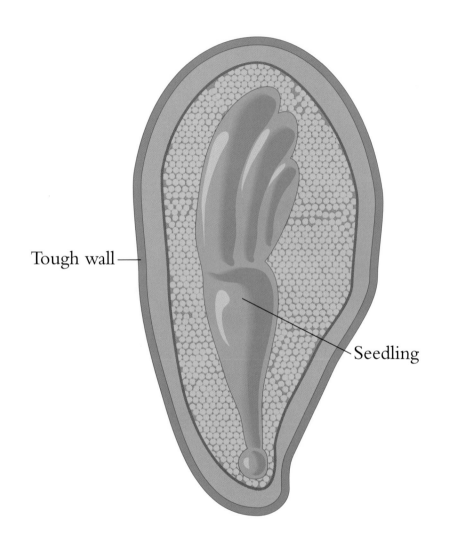

Tough wall

Seedling

The egg now becomes
a seed.

Inside the seed is the tiny
plant, or seedling, and
food for the seedling.

The seed grows a tough
wall around it.

The seedcase also changes. It may become the fruit of the plant, such as a watermelon or a pear.

Pears

The seedcase may also become a tough pod, such as a peapod or peanut shell.

The peas or peanuts inside are the seeds.

To become a new plant,
the seed takes a trip.

Small seeds are blown
by the wind. Some seeds
float in water.

Other seeds stick to the
fur of animals.

Dandelion seeds being blown by the wind

24

When the seed lands,
the trip is over.

The seed will need good
soil, water, and sunlight
to grow.

People plant seeds, too.

Farmers plant seeds to
raise new crops.

You might plant seeds
in your garden at home.

Isn't it amazing that these tall trees grew from tiny seeds?

Words You Know

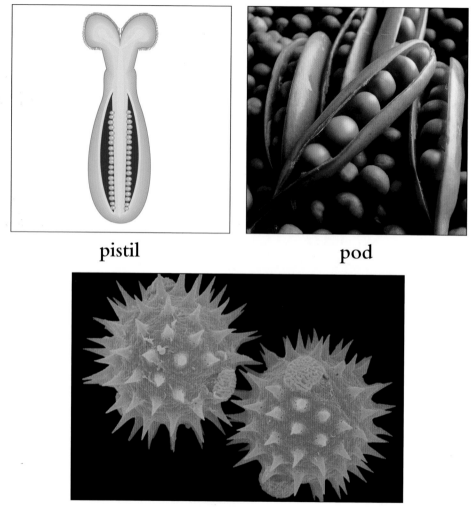

pistil

pod

pollen

seedcase

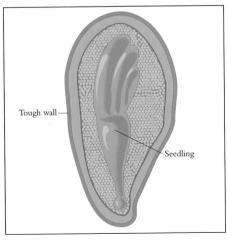

Tough wall

Seedling

seed

stamen

Index

animals, 22

crops, 26

eggs, 14, 15, 17

farmers, 26

flowers, 10, 12

foods, 3

fruit, 18, 19

garden, 26, 27

nectar, 12

peach pits, 7

pistil, 12, 13, 14

plants, 8, 9, 22

pod, 20, 21

pollen, 10, 12, 14, 15

pollen tube, 15

seedcase, 14, 15, 18, 19, 21

seedling, 16, 17

seeds, 3, 8, 10, 17, 21, 22, 23, 25, 26, 29

soil, 24, 25

stamen, 10, 11

sunlight, 25

tomato seeds, 4, 5

trees, 28, 29

wall, 16, 17

water, 22, 25

watermelon seeds, 6

wind, 22

About the Author

Allan Fowler is a freelance writer with a background in advertising.
Born in New York, he now lives in Chicago and enjoys traveling.

Photo Credits

Photographs ©: Envision: 20 top, 30 top (Paul Poplis); Photo Researchers:
3 top right (G. Buttner/Naturbild/OKAPIA), 10, 30 bottom (Andrew
Syred/SPL); PhotoEdit: 28 (D. Young-Wolff); Superstock, Inc.: 3 top left,
3 bottom, 6, 7, 19, 24, 31; Tony Stone Images: 9 (Val Corbett), 23 (Andy
Roberts), cover (Steve Taylor), 27 (Bob Thomas); Visuals Unlimited:
12 (Bill Beatty), 20 bottom (Jeff J. Daly), 4 (Wally Eberhart).

Illustrations by Mike DiGiorgio.